I0448741

Executive Summary

The National Protection Framework describes what the whole community should do to safeguard against acts of terrorism, natural disasters, and other threats or hazards. It describes the core capabilities; roles and responsibilities; and coordinating structures that facilitate the protection of individuals, communities, and the Nation. This Framework is focused on actions to protect against the greatest risks in a manner that allows American interests, aspirations, and way of life to thrive.

The Federal Government works collaboratively with local, state, tribal, and territorial governments; the private sector; and nongovernmental organizations (NGOs) to develop and deliver Protection core capabilities. Protection core capabilities are applied in varying degrees to achieve successful implementation of the Protection mission area.

The 11 core capabilities described in the National Protection Framework are Planning; Public Information and Warning; Operational Coordination; Access Control and Identity Verification; Cybersecurity; Intelligence and Information Sharing; Interdiction and Disruption; Physical Protective Measures; Risk Management for Protection Programs and Activities; Screening, Search and Detection; and Supply Chain Integrity and Security. The following principles guide the development and support the execution and deployment of Protection core capabilities. These guiding principles are resilience and scalability; risk-informed culture; and shared responsibility.

The National Protection Framework recognizes, values, and leverages the robust array of existing coordinating structures and identifies a protection cycle and guiding principles that promote integration and synchronization across the various jurisdictions and areas of responsibility. The range of coordinating structures that contribute to the Protection mission area includes, but is not limited to: operations centers; law enforcement task forces; critical infrastructure sector, government, and cross-sector coordinating councils; governance boards; regional consortiums; information sharing mechanisms, such as state and major urban area fusion centers; health surveillance networks; and public-private partnership organizations at all levels.

Protection capabilities are coordinated through existing partnerships at all levels of government and with the private sector and NGOs. These partnerships may cross critical infrastructure sector and geographical boundaries. They allow for the exchange of expertise and information and provide a source of potential resources through mutual aid and assistance agreements.

Partners across the whole community can use the National Protection Framework to inform and align relevant planning, training, exercising, and other activities designed to enhance security for individuals, families, communities, organizations, and jurisdictions. The protection processes and guiding principles contained in this Framework provide a structured and unifying approach that is flexible and adaptable to specific Protection mission requirements. Focusing planning, training, and exercises on the Protection core capabilities enhances preparedness over the long term.

The National Protection Framework provides individual, community, private sector, NGO, and governmental decision makers with an understanding of the spectrum of activities within the Protection mission area and what they can do to ensure our Nation is optimally protected from acts of terrorism and other threats or hazards. Initiatives based on Protection core capabilities help guide a community to create conditions for a safer, more secure, and more resilient Nation by enhancing protection through cooperation and collaboration.

In implementing the National Protection Framework to build national preparedness, partners are encouraged to develop a shared understanding of broad-level strategic implications as they make critical decisions in building future capacity and capability. The whole community should be engaged in examining and implementing the unifying principles and doctrine contained in this Framework, considering both current and future requirements in the process.

Table of Contents

Introduction

Presidential Policy Directive (PPD) 8: National Preparedness was released in March 2011 with the goal of strengthening the security and resilience of the United States through systematic preparation for the threats that pose the greatest risk to the security of the Nation. PPD-8 defines five preparedness mission areas—Prevention, Protection, Mitigation, Response, and Recovery—and mandates the development of a series of policy and planning documents to explain and guide the Nation's approach for ensuring and enhancing national preparedness. This National Protection Framework, part of the National Preparedness System, sets the strategy and doctrine for building, sustaining, and delivering the core capabilities for Protection identified in the National Preparedness Goal.

> **Prevention:** The capabilities necessary to avoid, prevent, or stop a threatened or actual act of terrorism. As defined by PPD-8, the term "prevention" refers to preventing imminent threats.
>
> **Protection:** The capabilities necessary to secure the homeland against acts of terrorism and manmade or natural disasters.
>
> **Mitigation:** The capabilities necessary to reduce loss of life and property by lessening the impact of disasters.
>
> **Response:** The capabilities necessary to save lives, protect property and the environment, and meet basic human needs after an incident has occurred.
>
> **Recovery:** The capabilities necessary to assist communities affected by an incident to recover effectively.

Framework Purpose and Organization

The National Protection Framework describes what the whole community—from community members to senior leaders in government—should do to safeguard against acts of terrorism, natural disasters, and other threats or hazards.[1] This Framework helps achieve the National Preparedness Goal of a secure and resilient Nation that is prepared to protect against the greatest risks in a manner that allows American interests, aspirations, and way of life to thrive. This Framework provides guidance to leaders and practitioners at all levels of government; the private and nonprofit sectors; and individuals by:

- Describing the core capabilities needed to achieve the Protection mission area and end-state of "creating conditions for a safer, more secure, and more resilient Nation"[2]

- Aligning key roles and responsibilities to deliver Protection capabilities

- Describing coordinating structures that enable all stakeholders to work together

---

[1] The whole community includes individuals, families, and households; communities; the private and nonprofit sectors; faith-based organizations; and local, state, tribal, territorial, and Federal governments. Whole community is defined in the National Preparedness Goal as "a focus on enabling the participation in national preparedness activities of a wider range of players from the private and nonprofit sectors, including nongovernmental organizations (NGOs) and the general public, in conjunction with the participation of Federal, state, and local governmental partners in order to foster better coordination and working relationships."

[2] The Protection end-state is defined in the National Preparedness Goal.

- Laying the foundation for further operational coordination and planning that will synchronize Protection efforts within the whole community and across the Prevention, Mitigation, Response, and Recovery mission areas.

The process and policies described in this document will be conducted in accordance with existing laws and regulations.

Intended Audience

The National Protection Framework describes how the whole community contributes to the spectrum of activities within the Protection mission area and what individuals and organizations can do to ensure the Nation is protected from all threats and hazards. Senior leaders with direct responsibility for implementing core capabilities within the Protection mission area should use this Framework as an accessible reference guide. Such leaders include, but are not limited to, government and corporate executives; law enforcement, security, public health, health systems, fire, emergency medical, and emergency management professionals; critical infrastructure owners and operators; and others with legal or statutory authorities within this mission area.

The National Protection Framework enables the whole community to contribute to and benefit from national preparedness by promoting the use of processes and coordinating mechanisms that provide equal access to acquire and use the necessary knowledge and skills. This includes children, individuals with disabilities, and others with access and functional needs;[3] those from diverse religious, racial, and ethnic backgrounds; and people with limited English proficiency. Their contributions must be integrated into preparedness efforts, and their needs must be incorporated during the planning and execution of the core capabilities.

Scope

Protection core capabilities are a key component of preparedness. The structures and capabilities needed to achieve the Protection mission area end-state build in large part upon existing doctrine, plans, and activities. The Protection mission area includes actions to deter threats, reduce vulnerabilities, or minimize the consequences associated with an incident. Effective protection relies upon the close coordination and alignment of practices across the whole community as well as with international partners and organizations.

The National Protection Framework focuses on Protection core capabilities that are applicable during both steady-state and enhanced steady-state conditions immediately before or during an incident. Steady-state conditions call for routine, normal, day-to-day operations. Enhanced steady-state conditions call for augmented operations that take place during temporary periods of heightened alert, during periods of incident response, or in support of planned events in which additional, or enhanced, protection activities are needed. This Framework addresses core capabilities that contribute to protecting the Nation domestically, but it does not address the protection of U.S. interests overseas.

---

[3] Access and functional needs includes ensuring the equal access and meaningful participation of all individuals, without discrimination.

The core capabilities for Protection enable a range of activities that include, but are not limited to:[4]

- **Critical Infrastructure Protection.** Protecting the physical and cyber elements of critical infrastructure. This includes actions to deter the threat, reduce vulnerabilities, or minimize the consequences associated with a terrorist attack, natural disaster, or manmade disaster. Critical Infrastructure Protection is an element of critical infrastructure security and resilience as detailed in Presidential Policy Directive 21: Critical Infrastructure Security and Resilience.[5]

- **Cybersecurity.** Securing the cyber environment and infrastructure from unauthorized or malicious access, use, or exploitation while protecting privacy, civil rights, and other civil liberties.

- **Defense Against Weapons of Mass Destruction (WMD) Threats.** Protecting the Nation from threats associated with WMD and related materials and technologies including their malicious acquisition, movement, and use within the United States.

- **Defense of Agriculture and Food**. Defending agriculture and food networks and systems from all-hazards threats and incidents.

- **Health Security.** Securing the Nation and its people to be prepared for, protected from, and resilient in the face of health threats or incidents with potentially negative health consequences.

- **Border Security.** Securing U.S. air, land, and sea ports and borders against the illegal flow of people and goods, while facilitating the flow of lawful travel and commerce.

- **Immigration Security.** Securing the Nation from illegal immigration through effective and efficient immigration systems and processes that respect human and civil rights.

- **Maritime Security.** Securing U.S. maritime infrastructure, resources, and the Marine Transportation System from terrorism and other threats and hazards and securing the homeland from an attack from the sea, while preserving civil rights, respecting privacy and protected civil liberties, and enabling legitimate travelers and goods to move efficiently without fear of harm or significant disruption.

- **Transportation Security.** Securing U.S. transportation systems and the air domain against terrorism and other threats and hazards, while preserving civil rights, respecting privacy and protected civil liberties, and enabling legitimate travelers and goods to move without fear of harm or significant disruption.

---

[4] As with all activities supporting the National Preparedness Goal, activities under the Protection mission area must be consistent with all pertinent statutes and policies, particularly those involving privacy and civil and human rights, such as the Americans with Disabilities Act of 1990, the Rehabilitation Act of 1973, and the Civil Rights Act of 1964.

[5] Critical infrastructure, as defined in PPD-21, includes those systems and assets, whether physical or virtual, so vital that the incapacity or destruction of such may have a debilitating impact on the security; economy; public safety or health; environment; or any combination of these matters, across any jurisdiction. Critical infrastructure security and resilience addresses sectors along common functions that include chemical; commercial facilities; communications; critical manufacturing; dams; defense industrial base; emergency services; energy; financial services; food and agriculture; government facilities; healthcare and public health; information technology; nuclear reactors, materials, and waste; transportation systems; and water and wastewater systems.

- **Protection of Key Leadership and Events**. Safeguarding government executive leadership from hostile acts by terrorists and other malicious actors and to ensure security at events of national significance.[6]

Guiding Principles

The following principles guide the development and support the execution and deployment of Protection core capabilities. These guiding principles are:

1. **Resilience and Scalability.** Effective delivery of the core capabilities for Protection minimizes the risks from all threats and hazards through:

   a. **Resilience.** Resilience may be enhanced through the delivery of core capabilities for Protection and involve a wide range of activities, including improving security protocols; hardening facilities; adopting redundancy; incorporating hazard resistance into facility design; initiating active or passive countermeasures; installing security systems; leveraging "self-healing" technologies; promoting workforce surety programs; implementing cybersecurity measures; training and exercises; business continuity planning; and restoration and recovery actions.[7]

   b. **Execution of scalable capabilities.** Scalable capabilities are designed to meet unforeseen, unmet, and evolving needs of varying geographic scope, complexity, and intensity.

2. **Risk-informed Culture.** A risk-informed culture supports Protection capabilities and requires:

   a. **Vigilance and situational awareness** through a comprehensive understanding of current, evolving, and emerging threats and hazards, as well as the relative risk they pose.

   b. **Information sharing and risk-informed decision making** through sharing appropriate, accessible, culturally and linguistically appropriate,[8] and timely information to allow for the ongoing analysis of risks and assessment of effective practices.

3. **Shared Responsibility.** Protection is most effective as a shared responsibility through:

   a. **Engaged partnerships** to exchange ideas, approaches, and effective practices; facilitate security planning and resource allocation; establish effective coordinating structures among partners; and build public awareness.

   b. **Integrated processes** across all levels of government and with private sector and NGO partners to more effectively achieve the shared vision of a safe and secure Nation.

---

[6] Key leaders are defined as current and former Presidents, Vice Presidents, their families, and others granted such protection under Title 18 U.S.C. Sections 3056 and 3056A. Events of national significance fall within two categories: National Special Security Events as defined in Title 18, U.S.C. Section 3056, and events assessed under the Special Event Assessment Rating process by the Department of Homeland Security (DHS) and the Federal Bureau of Investigation (FBI) based on input from Federal, state, and local law enforcement entities.

[7] The Protection and Mitigation mission areas work together to increase resilience. For an explanation of the differences and similarities between Protection and Mitigation, refer to the Core Capabilities section of this document.

[8] Information sharing must provide effective communication to individuals with disabilities and others with access and functional needs, including those who are deaf, hard of hearing, blind, or have low vision, through the use of appropriate auxiliary aids and services, such as sign language and other interpreters; captioning of audio and video materials; and user-accessible Web sites. In addition, information sharing should include communication in various languages and the use of culturally diverse media outlets.

Risk Basis

Risk is the potential for an unwanted outcome resulting from an incident, event, or occurrence, as determined by its likelihood and the associated consequences. It is assessed based on applicable threats and hazards, vulnerabilities, and consequences.

The Secretary of Homeland Security led an interagency effort to conduct a Strategic National Risk Assessment (SNRA) in support of PPD-8 in order to help identify the types of incidents that pose the greatest threat to the Nation's homeland security. The SNRA is useful in identifying the core capabilities essential to address these risks in each of the five preparedness mission areas— Prevention, Protection, Mitigation, Response, and Recovery—defined in the National Preparedness Goal. The National Protection Framework addresses the delivery of core capabilities required to protect against the threats identified in the SNRA shown in Table 1.

Table 1: National Threats and Hazards[9]

Threat/Hazard Group	Threat/Hazard Type
Natural	Animal Disease Outbreak
	Earthquake
	Flood
	Human Pandemic
	Hurricane
	Space Weather
	Tsunami
	Volcanic Eruption
	Wildfire
Technological/Accidental	Biological Food Contamination
	Chemical Substance Spill or Release
	Dam Failure
	Radiological Substance Release
Adversarial/Human-Caused	Aircraft as a Weapon
	Armed Assault
	Biological Terrorism Attack (non-food)
	Chemical/Biological Food Contamination Terrorism Attack
	Chemical Terrorism Attack (non-food)
	Cyber Attack Against Data
	Cyber Attack Against Physical Infrastructure
	Explosives Terrorism Attack
	Nuclear Terrorism Attack
	Radiological Terrorism Attack

For the purposes of the SNRA, the assessment focus is on contingency events, which typically are characterized by defined beginning and end points. The SNRA results enumerated in Table 1, however, do not explicitly assess a range of persistent steady-state risks, such as border and trade

---

[9] Source: SNRA (http://www.dhs.gov/xlibrary/assets/rma-strategic-national-risk-assessment-ppd8.pdf).

violations, illegal immigration, drug trafficking, and intellectual property violations, that account for a significant component of the steady-state Protection capabilities provided for by Federal departments and agencies. Furthermore, the efficient and effective processing of goods and people to and through the United States is a crucial part of the U.S. Government mission and is necessary to support the economy, promote job growth, and help partners in the trade community remain competitive in a constantly evolving world economy. Recognition of routine and ongoing Protection responsibilities along with the SNRA results guided the development of the National Protection Framework and should be considered by communities in their analysis.

Roles and Responsibilities

The whole community shares responsibility for maintaining awareness of threats and hazards and for taking actions to address risk. Many individuals, organizations, and entities engaged in the Protection mission area also key contributors across other mission areas. Protection partners have varying authorities, capacities, and resources that, when stitched together in a risk-informed way, provide the basis for the National Protection Framework.

Protection takes place across a continuum of conditions ranging from steady-state activities through enhanced steady-state. The National Protection Framework is designed to provide a cohesive and ongoing approach to dealing with those risks that can be most effectively managed through the delivery of the Protection core capabilities.

Individuals, Families, and Households

Individuals, families, and households provide the foundation for effective protection by maintaining awareness of threats and hazards and by taking risk-informed protective actions. Awareness of potential threats and hazards is acquired through an array of sources that include, but are not limited to: news outlets; public information and warning systems; and information sharing mechanisms, all of which are encouraged to be provided in a variety of accessible formats.

Communities

Communities are unified groups that share goals, values, or purposes, and may operate independently of geographic boundaries or jurisdictions. Communities bring individuals together in different ways for different reasons. They have the ability to promote and implement core capabilities within the Protection mission area and share information and effective practices. Communities may include faith-based organizations; neighborhood partnerships; communities representing or including those with disabilities and others with access and functional needs or those from diverse religious, racial, and ethnic backgrounds; online communities; hazard-specific or health coalitions; and professional associations.

Private Sector Entities

Private sector entities include businesses, industries, and private schools and universities. The focus for protection is on the owners and operators of the vast majority of the Nation's infrastructure. Owners and operators of both private and public sector infrastructure develop and implement risk-based protective programs and resilience strategies for the infrastructure and the related information and operations under their control.[10] Owners and operators maintain situational awareness and take actions on a continuous basis to build protection capabilities and make investments in security as necessary components of prudent day-to-day business and continuity of operations planning.

International Partnerships

While the National Protection Framework focuses on domestic activities, Protection capabilities often are interconnected globally. Protection efforts with foreign nations and regional and international organizations focus on instituting partnerships with international stakeholders, implementing agreements and instruments that affect protection, and addressing cross-sector and global issues. International partnerships are essential to developing and delivering core capabilities for the Protection mission area. Protection efforts with international partners require coordination with the Department of State and, as appropriate, other government entities at the Federal, state, tribal, and territorial levels.

Nongovernmental Organizations

NGOs are encouraged to establish or participate in regional and community preparedness partnerships with the whole community to develop a common understanding of risk and how to address it through their protection efforts. Where applicable, NGOs and faith-based organizations also contribute to the Protection mission area as advocates for, or assistance providers to, the entire range of community members by helping communities, individuals, and households to receive protection information and resources.

Local Governments

Local governments are responsible for the public safety, security, health, and welfare of the people who live in their jurisdictions. Local governments promote the coordination of ongoing protection plans and the implementation of core capabilities, as well as engagement and information sharing with private sector entities, infrastructure owners and operators, and other jurisdictions and regional entities. Local governments also address unique geographical protection issues, including transborder concerns, dependencies and interdependencies among agencies and enterprises, and, as necessary, the establishment of agreements for cross-jurisdictional and public-private coordination. Local governments are also responsible for ensuring all citizens receive timely information in a variety of accessible formats.

State, Tribal, Territorial, and Insular Area Governments

State, tribal, territorial, and insular area governments are also responsible for implementing the homeland security mission, protecting public welfare, and ensuring the provision of essential services and information to protect public health and security to communities and infrastructure within their jurisdictions. Similar to local governments, they address transborder issues and organizational interdependencies, and establish coordination agreements. These levels of government serve an integral role as a conduit for vertical coordination between Federal agencies and local governments.

---

[10] For the purposes of the National Protection Framework, "owners and operators" includes owners and operators both of privately owned businesses and infrastructure as well as publicly owned infrastructure (e.g., public works and utilities).

Federal Government

The President leads the Federal Government protection efforts to prepare the Nation for all hazards, including natural disasters, acts of terrorism, and other emergencies. The Federal Government provides leadership, coordination, and integration for the development and delivery of Protection capabilities. Federal departments and agencies execute national policy directives and implement statutory and regulatory responsibilities for a wide array of protective programs and provide assistance in a number of areas, including funding, acquisition, research, coordination, oversight, implementation, and enforcement.

All Federal departments and agencies must cooperate with one another, and with local, state, tribal, territorial, and insular area governments, community members, NGOs, and the private sector to the maximum extent possible. The Federal Government, working with all of these partners, contributes to the development and delivery of the core capabilities by establishing and implementing national laws, regulations, guidelines, and standards designed to protect the public while ensuring the free flow of commerce and the protection of privacy, civil rights, and civil liberties. The Federal Government provides integrated public safety and security capabilities and resources for potential or actual incidents requiring a coordinated Federal response.

A range of Federal departments and agencies have differing responsibilities regarding protection. The Protection Federal Interagency Operational Plan (FIOP) will provide a detailed description of how the following Federal departments and agencies engage and contribute to the delivery of core capabilities:[11]

- Department of Homeland Security[12]

- Department of Agriculture

- Department of Defense

- Department of Energy

- Department of Health and Human Services[13]

---

[11] The FIOPs are a required component of the National Preparedness System directed under PPD-8. Their intent is to provide guidance across the Federal Government to successfully implement the frameworks. The Protection FIOP is discussed further in the Operational Planning section of this document.

[12] By directive of the President, the Secretary of Homeland Security is the principal Federal official for domestic incident management. Pursuant to the Homeland Security Act of 2002, the Secretary is the focal point regarding natural and manmade crises and emergency planning. The primary DHS mission is to prevent terrorist attacks within the United States; reduce the vulnerability of the United States to terrorism; and to minimize the damage and assist in the recovery from terrorist attacks that do occur within the United States. In order to protect against, mitigate, and, when appropriate, prevent terrorist attacks, major disasters, and other emergencies, the Secretary is responsible for identifying strategic priorities and coordinating domestic all-hazards preparedness efforts of Executive Branch departments and agencies, in consultation with local, state, tribal, and territorial governments, NGOs, private sector partners, and the general public (except for those activities that may interfere with the authority of the Attorney General or the FBI Director, as described in PPD-8). The National Operations Center is the principal operations center for DHS.

[13] The Pandemic and All-Hazards Preparedness Act directs the Secretary of Health and Human Services to develop a National Health Security Strategy with a focus on human health. In addition to the departments and agencies listed here for their unique roles in human, animal, and environmental health, the National Health Security Strategy is supported by the Departments of Homeland Security, Defense, Education, Justice, Labor, State, and Transportation; the Federal Communications Commission; the Office of Personnel Management; and the Executive Office of the President.

- Department of the Interior
- Department of Justice[14]
- Department of State[15]
- Department of Transportation
- Department of the Treasury
- Environmental Protection Agency
- General Services Administration
- Office of the Director of National Intelligence.[16]

The authority for the Protection mission is established in local, state, tribal, territorial, and Federal laws, regulations, ordinances, and other directives with the force and effect of law. National policy

---

[14] Like other Executive Branch departments and agencies, the Department of Justice and the FBI will endeavor to coordinate their activities with other members of the law enforcement community, and with members of the Intelligence Community, to achieve maximum cooperation consistent with the law and operational necessity. The Attorney General has lead responsibility for criminal investigations of terrorist acts or terrorist threats, where such acts are within the Federal criminal jurisdiction of the United States, as well as for related intelligence collection activities within the United States, subject to the National Security Act of 1947 (as amended) and other applicable law, Executive Order 12333 (as amended), and Attorney General-approved procedures to that Executive Order. Generally acting through the FBI Director, the Attorney General, in cooperation with Federal departments and agencies engaged in activities to protect our national security, shall also coordinate the activities of the other members of the law enforcement community to detect, prevent, preempt, and disrupt terrorist attacks against the United States. Generally acting through the FBI Director, the Attorney General has primary responsibility for finding and neutralizing WMDs within the United States. The FBI Director exercises lead agency responsibility in investigating all crimes for which it has primary or concurrent jurisdiction and that involve terrorist activities or acts in preparation of terrorist activities within the statutory jurisdiction of the United States. Within the United States, this responsibility includes the collection, coordination, analysis, management, and dissemination of intelligence and criminal information in collaboration with other Executive Branch departments as appropriate. Relating to any foreign counterintelligence matter, the FBI Director is designated by Presidential directives to take charge of investigative work regarding espionage, sabotage, subversive activities, and other foreign counterintelligence matters. Working with other Departments when appropriate, the Attorney General, generally acting through the FBI Director, will reduce domestic terrorist threats, thwart, and investigate attacks on or criminal disruptions of critical infrastructure and key resources. The Attorney General and the Secretary of Homeland Security shall use applicable statutory authority and attendant mechanisms for cooperation and coordination, including but not limited to those established by Presidential directive. Following a terrorist threat or an actual incident that falls within the criminal jurisdiction of the United States, the full capabilities of the United States shall be dedicated, consistent with U.S. law and with activities of other Federal departments and agencies to protect our national security, to assist the Attorney General to identify the perpetrators and bring them to justice. The Strategic Information and Operations Center acts as the FBI's worldwide emergency operations center.

[15] As part of the day-to-day diplomatic activities on behalf of the U.S. Government, the Department of State is responsible for establishing and maintaining international partnerships which are essential to developing and delivering core capabilities for the Protection mission area.

[16] The Director of National Intelligence serves as the head of the Intelligence Community, acts as the principal advisor to the President for intelligence matters relating to national security, and oversees and directs implementation of the National Intelligence Program. The Intelligence Community, comprising elements across the Federal Government, functions consistent with law, executive order, regulations, and policy to support the national security-related missions of the U.S. Government. In addition to Intelligence Community elements with specific homeland security missions, the Office of the Director of National Intelligence maintains a number of mission and support centers that provide unique capabilities, which together support the delivery of all the core capabilities for Protection.

directives and regulations direct Federal agencies to conduct protection activities within and across several critical infrastructure sectors. The National Protection Framework does not change or replace any existing responsibilities and authorities as specified by law, directive, or policy. Federal departments and agencies are required by law to ensure accessible communication, physical access, and programmatic access to ensure all citizens have equal access and equal opportunity.

Core Capabilities

The National Preparedness Goal identifies the core capabilities and targets for each of the five mission areas. Table 2 provides a list of the core capabilities by mission area. Many of these core capabilities exist and are used every day for steady-state protection activities. The approach to further developing and delivering these core capabilities will differ according to and across the mission areas.

Table 2: Core Capabilities by Mission Area[17]

Prevention	Protection	Mitigation	Response	Recovery
Planning				
Public Information and Warning				
Operational Coordination				
Intelligence and Information Sharing	Intelligence and Information Sharing	Community Resilience	Critical Transportation	Economic Recovery
Interdiction and Disruption	Interdiction and Disruption	Long-Term Vulnerability Reduction	Environmental Response/ Health and Safety	Health and Social Services
Screening, Search, and Detection	Screening, Search, and Detection	Risk and Disaster Resilience Assessment	Fatality Management Services	Housing
Forensics and Attribution	Access Control and Identity Verification	Threat and Hazard Identification	Infrastructure Systems	Infrastructure Systems
	Cybersecurity		Mass Care Services	Natural and Cultural Resources
	Physical Protective Measures		Mass Search and Rescue Operations	
	Risk Management for Protection Programs and Activities		On-Scene Security and Protection	
	Supply Chain Integrity and Security		Operational Communications	
			Public and Private Services and Resources	
			Public Health and Medical Services	
			Situational Assessment	

The National Preparedness Goal identifies 11 core capabilities for the Protection mission area. Three of these core capabilities—Planning, Public Information and Warning, and Operational

---

[17] The National Preparedness Goal outlines the core capabilities for each mission area.

Coordination—cross-cut all of the mission areas. In addition, the Protection and Prevention mission areas share three core capabilities: Intelligence and Information Sharing; Interdiction and Disruption; and Screening, Search, and Detection. The cross-cutting core capabilities between mission areas provide opportunities for integration. Prevention and Protection use many of the same capabilities and coordinating structures, including for delivering Intelligence and Information Sharing; Interdiction and Disruption; and Screening, Search, and Detection. Protection and Mitigation share capabilities directly related to risk management. For Protection, the capability is Risk Management for Protection Programs and Activities. For Mitigation, risk management is informed by Long-Term Vulnerability Reduction; Risk and Disaster Resilience Assessment; and Threat and Hazard Identification. The Protection and Mitigation mission areas coordinate through the risk management process as they identify threats and hazards and work to reduce vulnerabilities. Figure 1 is a simplified graphic that conceptually illustrates the interconnectedness of all of the mission areas. The figure calls specific attention to the connections and shared or related core capabilities that align efforts in the context of Protection and Prevention, as well as Protection and Mitigation. Additionally, Protection is linked to Response and Recovery through various core capabilities such as those pertaining to Infrastructure Systems and relevant coordinating structures.

Figure 1: Protection and Integrated Core Capabilities

Collectively, the core capabilities for the Protection mission area provide the foundation for achieving the overarching critical objective for Protection: a homeland that is protected from terrorism and other hazards in a manner that allows American interests, aspirations, and way of life to thrive. The National Preparedness Goal established preliminary targets for each of the Protection mission area core capabilities.[18] The targets from the Goal were used to identify critical tasks, listed on the following pages. The critical tasks are specific to Protection and can be used to identify tailored goals and objectives.

The critical tasks associated with the Protection core capabilities are ambitious. They are not tasks for any single jurisdiction or agency; rather, achieving them will require a national effort involving the whole community.

Cross-cutting Core Capabilities

The following three core capabilities span all five mission areas: Planning, Public Information and Warning, and Operational Coordination.

Planning

Description: Conducting a systematic process that engages the whole community, as appropriate, in the development of executable strategic, operational, or community-based approaches to meet defined Protection objectives.

Planning includes the development of multidisciplinary plans; their implementation, exercising, and maintenance; and the promotion of planning initiatives.

Critical Tasks:

- Initiate a flexible planning process that builds on existing plans.

- Establish partnerships, facilitate coordinated information sharing between partners, and enable the planning and protection of critical infrastructure within the jurisdiction.

- Implement measures to identify and prioritize critical infrastructure and determine risk.

- Conduct vulnerability assessments, perform risk analyses, identify capability gaps, and coordinate protective measures on an ongoing basis in conjunction with the private sector and local, state, tribal, territorial, and Federal organizations and agencies.

- Implement security, protection, resilience, and continuity plans and programs, train and exercise, and take corrective actions.

- Develop and implement progress measures and communicate adjustments and improvements to applicable stakeholders and authorities.

- Integrate planning for the whole community, including, but not limited to, individuals with disabilities and others with access and functional needs, as well as those with limited English proficiency, and racially and ethnically diverse communities.

Public Information and Warning

Description: Delivering coordinated, prompt, reliable, and actionable information to the whole community through the use of clear, consistent, accessible, and culturally and linguistically appropriate methods. These efforts will be implemented to effectively relay information regarding any threat or hazard and, as appropriate, the actions being taken and the assistance made available.

---

[18] The Protection mission area capabilities and preliminary targets are identified in the National Preparedness Goal.

Public Information and Warning uses effective and accessible indications and warning systems to communicate significant threats and hazards to involved operators, security officials, and the public (including alerts, detection capabilities, and other necessary and appropriate assets).[19]

Critical Tasks:

- Determine requirements for protection stakeholder information and information sharing.

- Determine information sharing requirements and processes to address the communication needs of children; people with limited English proficiency; and individuals with disabilities and others with access and functional needs, including those who are deaf, hard of hearing, blind, or have low vision through the use of appropriate auxiliary aids and services, such as sign language and other interpreters and the captioning of audio and video materials.

- Establish accessible mechanisms and provide the full spectrum of support necessary for appropriate and ongoing information sharing among all levels of government, the private sector, faith-based organizations, NGOs, and the public.

- Promptly share actionable measures with the public and among all levels of government, the private sector, and NGOs.

- Leverage all appropriate communication means, such as the Integrated Public Alert and Warning System, National Terrorism Advisory System, and social media sites and technology.

Operational Coordination

Description: Establishing and maintaining unified and coordinated operational structures and processes that appropriately integrate all critical stakeholders and support the execution of core capabilities.

Operational Coordination supports networking, planning, and coordination between protection partners.

Critical Tasks:

- Collaborate with all relevant protection partners.

- Determine jurisdictional priorities, objectives, strategies, and resource allocations.

- Establish clear lines and modes of communication among participating organizations and jurisdictions.

- Define and communicate clear roles and responsibilities relative to courses of action.

- Integrate and synchronize the actions of participating organizations and jurisdictions to ensure unity of effort.

- Determine requirements for protection stakeholder operational coordination.

- Coordinate across and among all levels of government and with critical nongovernmental and private sector partners to protect against potential threats, conduct law enforcement investigations, or engage in enforcement and protective activities based on jurisdictional authorities.

---

[19] Public information and warning systems must provide effective communication to individuals with disabilities, such as through audio and video captioning for multimedia and use-accessible Web sites. Information and warning should also be communicated using various languages and culturally diverse media outlets.

- Coordinate with the appropriate partners in other mission areas.

Protection and Prevention Core Capabilities

The following core capabilities span the Protection and Prevention mission areas: Intelligence and Information Sharing; Interdiction and Disruption; and Screening, Search, and Detection.

Intelligence and Information Sharing

Description: Intelligence sharing is providing timely, accurate, and actionable information resulting from intelligence processes concerning threats to the United States, its people, property, or interests; the development, proliferation, or use of WMDs; or any other matter bearing on U.S. national or homeland security by local, state, tribal, territorial, Federal, and other stakeholders.[20] **Information sharing** is the capability to exchange intelligence and other information; data; or knowledge among local, state, tribal, territorial, Federal, or private sector entities, or international partners as appropriate.

All actions in the National Protection Framework begin with the monitoring, gathering, and analysis of intelligence and information. Intelligence and information sharing may use pre-defined networks, procedures, and formats.

In the context of Protection and Prevention, Intelligence and Information Sharing capabilities involve the effective implementation of the intelligence cycle and other information collection and sharing processes by local, state, tribal, territorial, and Federal entities, the private sector, NGOs, and the public to develop situational awareness of potential threats and hazards within the United States.

Lawful sharing of information with robust and collaborative partnerships, coupled with coordinated interactions that increase situational awareness, strengthen the Protection mission. The U.S. Government promotes an information sharing culture, deploys new technologies, and refines its policies and procedures in support of its commitment to share timely, relevant, and actionable intelligence and other information to the widest appropriate audience.

Critical Tasks:

- Monitor, detect, and analyze threats and hazards to public safety, health, and security, which include:

  - Participation in local, state, tribal, territorial, regional, and national education and awareness programs.

  - Participation in the routine exchange of security information—including threat assessments, alerts, attack indications and warnings, and advisories—among partners.

- Determine requirements for protection stakeholder intelligence, information, and information sharing.

---

[20] Intelligence processes include the following steps: planning; direction; the collection, exploitation, processing, and analysis of available information; production; dissemination; evaluation; and feedback.

- Develop or identify and provide access to mechanisms and procedures for intelligence and information sharing between the public, private sector, faith-based, and government protection partners.[21]

- Using intelligence processes, produce and deliver relevant, timely, accessible, and actionable intelligence and information products to others as applicable, to include partners in the other mission areas.

- Adhere to appropriate mechanisms for safeguarding sensitive and classified information.

Interdiction and Disruption

Description: Delaying, diverting, intercepting, halting, apprehending, or securing threats and/or hazards.

These threats and hazards include people, materials, or activities that pose a threat to the Nation, including domestic and transnational criminal and terrorist activities and the malicious movement and acquisition/transfer of chemical, biological, radiological, nuclear, and explosive (CBRNE) materials and related technologies.

In the context of Protection and Prevention, this capability includes those interdiction and disruption activities undertaken in response to specific, actionable intelligence that indicates the location of a suspected weapon or threat actor or material.[22] It might also include urgent activities required when an imminent threat is encountered unexpectedly.

Interdiction and disruption activities conducted by law enforcement and public and private sector security personnel during the course of their routine duties include the enforcement of border authorities at and between ports of entry into the United States.

Critical Tasks:

- Prevent movement and operation of terrorists into or within the United States and its territories.

- Ensure the capacity to detect and render safe CBRNE devices or resolve CBRNE threats.

- Interdict conveyances, cargo, and persons associated with a potential threat or act.

- Implement public health measures to mitigate the spread of disease threats abroad and prevent disease threats from crossing national borders.

- Disrupt terrorist financing or conduct counter-acquisition activities to prevent weapons, precursors, related technology, or other material support from reaching its target.

- Enhance the visible presence of law enforcement to deter or disrupt threats from reaching potential target(s).

- Employ wide-area search and detection assets in targeted areas in concert with local, state, tribal, and territorial personnel or other Federal agencies (depending on the threat).

---

[21] Information sharing must provide effective communication to individuals with disabilities and others with access and functional needs, including those who are deaf, hard of hearing, blind, or have low vision, through the use of appropriate auxiliary aids and services, such as sign language and other interpreters, captioning of audio and video materials and user-accessible Web sites. Information sharing also should include communication in various languages and use of culturally diverse media outlets.

[22] Interdiction and disruption activities specifically undertaken to resolve an imminent threat and prevent actual terrorist attacks and follow-on attacks are addressed in the National Prevention Framework and Prevention FIOP.

Screening, Search, and Detection

Description: Identifying, discovering, or locating threats and/or hazards through active and passive surveillance and search procedures. These activities may include the use of systematic examinations and assessments, sensor technologies, disease surveillance, laboratory testing, or physical investigation and intelligence.

In the context of Protection and Prevention, this capability includes the screening of cargo, conveyances, mail, baggage, and people, as well as the detection of WMD, traditional, and emerging threats and hazards of concern.

Screening, search, and detection actions safeguard citizens, residents, visitors, and critical assets, systems, and networks against the most dangerous threats to the Nation without unduly hampering commerce.

Critical Tasks:

- Locate persons and criminal/terrorist networks associated with a potential threat.

- Develop and engage an observant Nation (individuals, families, communities, and local, state, tribal, and territorial government and private sector partners).

- Screen persons, baggage, mail, cargo, and conveyances using technical, non-technical, intrusive, and non-intrusive means without unduly hampering the flow of legitimate commerce. Consider additional measures for high-risk persons, conveyances, or items.

  - Conduct CBRNE search and detection operations.

  - Conduct ambient and active detection of CBRNE agents.

  - Operate safely in a hazardous environment.

  - Consider the deployment of Federal teams and capabilities to enhance local, state, tribal, and territorial efforts, including the use of incident assessment and awareness assets.

- Conduct biosurveillance of data relating to human health, animal, plant, food, water, and environmental domains.

Core Capabilities Unique to Protection

The remaining core capabilities are unique to Protection: Access Control and Identity Verification; Cybersecurity; Physical Protective Measures; Risk Management for Protection Programs and Activities; and Supply Chain Integrity and Security.

Access Control and Identity Verification

Description: Applying a broad range of physical, technological, and cyber measures to control admittance to critical locations and systems, limiting access to authorized individuals to carry out legitimate activities.

This capability relies on the implementation and maintenance of protocols to verify identity and authorize, grant, or deny physical and cyber access to specific locations, information, and networks.

Critical Tasks:

- Verify identity to authorize, grant, or deny physical and cyber access to physical and cyber assets, networks, applications, and systems that could be exploited to do harm.

- Control and limit access to critical locations and systems to authorized individuals carrying out legitimate activities.

Cybersecurity

Description: Protecting against damage to, unauthorized use of, and/or malicious exploitation of (and, if needed, the restoration of) information and communications technologies (and the data contained therein).

Cybersecurity activities ensure the security, reliability, integrity, and availability of critical information, records, and communications systems and services through collaborative cybersecurity initiatives and efforts.

Critical Tasks:

- Implement countermeasures, technologies, and policies to protect physical and cyber assets, networks, applications, and systems that could be exploited to do harm.

- Secure, to the extent possible, public and private networks and critical infrastructure (e.g., communication, financial, power grid, water, and transportation systems), based on vulnerability results from risk assessment, mitigation, and incident response capabilities.

- Share actionable cyber threat information with the domestic and international, government, and private sectors to promote shared situational awareness.

- Implement risk-informed standards to ensure the security, reliability, integrity, and availability of critical information, records, and communications systems and services through collaborative cybersecurity initiatives and efforts.

- Detect and analyze malicious activity and support mitigation activities.

- Collaborate with partners to develop plans and processes to facilitate coordinated incident response activities.

- Leverage law enforcement and intelligence assets to identify, track, investigate, disrupt, and prosecute malicious actors threatening the security of the Nation's public and private information systems.

Physical Protective Measures

Description: Reducing or mitigating risks, including actions targeted at threats, vulnerabilities, and/or consequences, by controlling movement and protecting borders, critical infrastructure, and the homeland.

This capability includes the development, implementation, and maintenance of risk-informed physical protections, countermeasures, and policies protecting people, structures, materials, products, and systems associated with key operational activities and critical infrastructure sectors.

Critical Tasks:

- Identify and prioritize assets, systems, networks, and functions that need to be protected.

- Identify needed physical protections, countermeasures, and policies through a risk assessment of key operational activities and infrastructure.

- Develop and implement security plans, including business continuity plans, that address identified security risks.

- Develop and implement risk-based physical security measures, countermeasures, policies, and procedures.

- Implement security training for workers, focused on awareness and response.

- Develop and implement biosecurity and biosafety programs and practices.

- Leverage Federal acquisition programs, as appropriate, to ensure maximum cost efficiency, security, and interoperability of procurements.

Risk Management for Protection Programs and Activities

(Aligned with Mitigation)

Description: Identifying, assessing, and prioritizing risks to inform Protection activities and investments.

This goal is accomplished by implementing and maintaining risk assessment processes to identify and prioritize assets, systems, networks, and functions, as well as implementing and maintaining appropriate tools to identify and assess threats, vulnerabilities, and consequences.

Risk management is a systemic and analytical process to consider the likelihood that a threat will endanger an asset, individual, or function and to identify actions to reduce the risk and mitigate the consequences. Threat assessments are a decision support tool that can assist in security program planning. Threat assessments identify and provide an evaluation of threats based on various factors, including capability and intentions, as well as the potential lethality and other consequences of an attack.

Critical Tasks:

- Gather required data in a timely and accurate manner to effectively identify risks.

- Obtain and use appropriate threat, vulnerability, and consequence tools to identify and assess threats, vulnerabilities, and consequences.

- Build the capability within communities to analyze and assess risk and resilience.

- Identify, implement, and monitor risk management plans.

- Update risk assessments to reassess risk based on changes in the following areas: the physical environment, aging infrastructure, new development, new mitigation projects and initiatives, post-event verification/validation, new technologies or improved methodologies, and better or more up-to-date data.

- Validate, calibrate, and enhance risk assessments by relying on experience, lessons learned, and knowledge beyond raw data or models.

- Use risk assessments to design exercises and determine the feasibility of mitigation projects and initiatives.

- Engage in a peer-to-peer mentoring structure that promotes effective practices.

Supply Chain Integrity and Security

Description: Strengthening the security and resilience of the supply chain.

This capability relies on securing and making resilient key nodes, methods of transport between nodes, and materials in transit between a supplier and consumer.

The expansive nature of the global supply chain renders it vulnerable to disruption from intentional or naturally occurring causes. The multimodal, international nature of the global supply chain system requires a broad effort that includes input from stakeholders from the public and private sectors, both international and domestic. Protection relies on a layered, risk-based, and balanced approach in which necessary security measures and resiliency planning are integrated into supply chains.

Critical Tasks:

- Integrate security processes into supply chain operations to identify items of concern and resolve them as early in the process as possible.

- Analyze key dependencies and interdependencies related to supply chain operations.[23]

- Use risk management principles to identify, mitigate vulnerabilities of, and protect key assets, infrastructure, and support systems.

- Implement physical protections, countermeasures, and policies to secure and make resilient key nodes, methods of transport between nodes, and materials in transit.

- Use verification and detection capabilities to identify goods that are not what they are represented to be, are contaminated, are not declared, or are prohibited; and to prevent cargo from being compromised or misdirected as it moves through the system.

- Use layers of defense to protect against a diverse range of traditional and asymmetric threats. These layers include: intelligence and information analysis; appropriate use of technology; effective laws, regulations, and policies; properly trained and equipped personnel; and effective partnerships.

Coordinating Structures and Integration

Coordinating structures provide the mechanisms to develop and deliver core capabilities. Coordinating structures across the whole community provide for the flexible, scalable, and adaptable approach to the delivery of core capabilities identified in PPD-8. The National Protection Framework recognizes, values, and leverages the robust array of existing coordinating structures, and identifies a protection cycle and guiding principles that promote integration and synchronization across the various jurisdictions and areas of responsibility.

In the context of the National Protection Framework, coordinating structures support protection program implementation and strengthen the Nation's ability to increase the protective posture when required to augment operations that take place during temporary periods of heightened alert, during periods of incident response, or in support of planned events. These structures are used to conduct planning, implement training and exercise programs, promote information sharing, shape research and development priorities and technical requirements, address common vulnerabilities, align resources, and promote the delivery of Protection capabilities.

The range of coordinating structures that contribute to the Protection mission area includes, but is not limited to: operations centers; law enforcement task forces; critical infrastructure partnerships; governance boards; regional consortiums; information sharing mechanisms such as state and major

---

[23] Dependency is a one-directional reliance on input, interaction, or another source in order to function properly. Interdependency is a mutually reliant relationship between objects, individuals, or groups. The degree of interdependency does not need to be equal in both directions.

urban area fusion centers; health surveillance networks; and public-private partnership organizations at all levels.

Community, Local, State, and Regional Coordinating Structures

Coordination through Partnerships

Protection mission capabilities are coordinated through existing partnerships at all levels of government and with the private sector and NGOs. There are numerous examples of existing protection partnerships or coalitions, ranging from neighborhood-based programs to regional public-private councils, joint task forces, healthcare coalitions, and infrastructure protection coordinating councils. Many established community and regional groups promote actions to support protection and preparedness. These partnerships may cross critical infrastructure sectors and geographical boundaries. They allow for the exchange of expertise and information and provide a source of potential resources through mutual aid and assistance agreements.

PPD-21, for example, promotes the shared responsibility for critical infrastructure security and resilience efforts among all levels of government and critical infrastructure owners and operators. While not the only public-private partnership in the U.S. Government, this partnership focuses on the security and resilience of critical infrastructure. Sector-specific agencies (SSAs) are responsible for critical infrastructure security and resilience activities in specified sectors.[24] Each sector has built partnerships with sector stakeholders, including facility owners and operators; local, state, tribal, territorial, and Federal Government agencies; the law enforcement community; trade associations; and state homeland security advisors. The established sector, government, and cross-sector councils and information sharing mechanisms, such as Information Sharing and Analysis Centers, are among the foundational structures for protection planning, risk management, and the implementation of protective programs. SSAs are responsible for working with both public and private partners to develop security and resilience programs and strategies.

Because of the specific challenges and interdependencies facing individual regions and the broad range and diversity of public and private sector partners and NGOs, regional efforts are often complex. Examples of regional partnerships formed to consider regional issues range from the Pacific NorthWest Economic Region (PNWER) partnership,[25] whose working groups look at such issues as border security, agriculture, and energy, to regional partnerships that focus primarily on a single infrastructure sector, such as the Multi-state Partnership for Security in Agriculture.[26]

Voluntary public/private collaboration and information sharing between public and private sector partners and NGOs is essential to meeting critical objectives for core capabilities within the Protection mission area and sustaining programs.

---

[24] The SSAs responsible for critical infrastructure security and resilience for specified sectors are identified in PPD-21: Critical Infrastructure Security and Resilience. PPD-21 also provides that, in addition to the responsibilities given to the SSAs, other Federal departments and agencies have special functions relating to critical infrastructure security and resilience.

[25] Founded in 1991, PNWER is a statutory, bi-national, public/private partnership. PNWER facilitates working groups of public and private leaders to address issues impacting the Pacific Northwest regional economy.

[26] Founded in 2004, the Multi-State Partnership for Security in Agriculture is a 14-state consortium that recognizes that agricultural disasters could have regional, national, and global effects.

Operational Coordination

In most jurisdictions, local operations centers are the focal point for coordinating the delivery of Protection capabilities to the whole community. In addition, state and major urban fusion centers support and inform operational coordination by serving as focal points within the state and local environments for the receipt, analysis, gathering, and sharing of threat-related information between government, NGOs, and private sector partners. DHS coordinates critical infrastructure security and resilience activities through the National Infrastructure Coordinating Center and the National Cybersecurity and Communications Integration Center. Joint Terrorism Task Forces are FBI-led multijurisdictional task forces established to conduct terrorism-related investigations and are based in 103 cities nationwide. FBI Joint Terrorism Task Forces focus primarily on terrorism-related issues, with specific regard to terrorism investigations with local, regional, national, and international implications. Coordination with FBI Joint Terrorism Task Forces and information sharing with operations and fusion centers help inform Prevention, Protection, Response, and Recovery activities. These centers also contribute insights and lessons learned to shape Mitigation planning efforts.

Coordination through Established Systems and Principles

The National Protection Framework promotes the use of principles such as those contained in the National Incident Management System to coordinate core capabilities within the Protection mission area across all levels of government, the private sector, and NGOs. The National Incident Management System, for example, provides guidelines to enable organizations with different legal, geographic, and functional responsibilities to coordinate, plan, and interact effectively. Each participating organization maintains its authority, responsibility, and accountability. The National Incident Management System components, concepts, and principles support the transition of organizations that have active roles in multiple mission areas.

Federal Coordinating Structures

At the Federal level, an array of coordinating structures exist to facilitate partnerships, planning, information sharing, and resource and operational synchronization across all aspects of the Protection mission area. This section focuses on the policy-level coordination conducted through White House leadership, public-private partnerships, and those structures that are in place or need to be established to ensure a coordinated approach to protection across the whole community.

National Security Council

The National Security Council is the principal policy body for consideration of national security policy issues requiring Presidential determination. The National Security Council advises and assists the President in integrating all aspects of national security policy as it affects the United States— domestic, foreign, military, intelligence, and economic (in conjunction with the National Economic Council). Along with its subordinate committees, the National Security Council is the President's principal means for coordinating Executive Branch departments and agencies in the development and implementation of national security policy.

Federal Departments and Agencies

In addition to the Secretary of Homeland Security's statutory and other responsibilities, PPD-8 states "the Secretary of Homeland Security is responsible for coordinating the domestic all-hazards preparedness efforts of all Executive Branch departments and agencies, in consultation with state, local, tribal, and territorial governments, NGOs, private-sector partners, and the general public."[27] PPD-8 further states that the heads of all Executive Branch departments and agencies with a role in Protection are responsible for national preparedness efforts consistent with their statutory roles and responsibilities.[28]

The Federal Government promotes coordination within the Protection mission area through a wide range of coordinating structures. Under the National Protection Framework, various Federal departments or agencies assume primary coordinating roles based on their authorities and the nature of the threat or hazard. These Federal departments and agencies provide the basis for the ongoing coordination and collaboration that will be required to promote implementation and ensure the ongoing management and maintenance of the National Protection Framework and other Protection preparedness requirements established through PPD-8.

The Secretary of Homeland Security will convene, as appropriate, a meeting or meetings among Federal department and agency representatives to discuss and consider the coordination of core capabilities within the Protection mission area, focusing on the following:

- Preparedness planning and coordination in accordance with the National Protection Framework and other PPD-8 implementation efforts

- Information sharing pertinent to protection activities

- Collaboration across the whole community

- Common concerns and recommended courses of action

- Integration with Prevention, Mitigation, Response, and Recovery by coordinating with similar groups within those mission areas.

Steady-state Protection Process

This section summarizes the process to identify the measures necessary to protect against threats and hazards under steady-state conditions. The responsibility for steady-state protection is shared by the protection community, including individuals and their households, all levels of government, NGOs, and the private sector.

All entities that are responsible for protection—including governments at all levels, critical infrastructure owners and operators, and businesses—are encouraged to use the steady-state coordinating process to identify the core capabilities needed to accomplish the Protection mission. Figure 2 depicts the steady-state protection process.

---

[27] Except for those activities that may interfere with the authority of the Attorney General or the FBI Director, as described in PPD-8 and PPD-21.
[28] Specific statutory and other responsibilities of Federal departments and agencies are identified in the Roles and Responsibilities section.

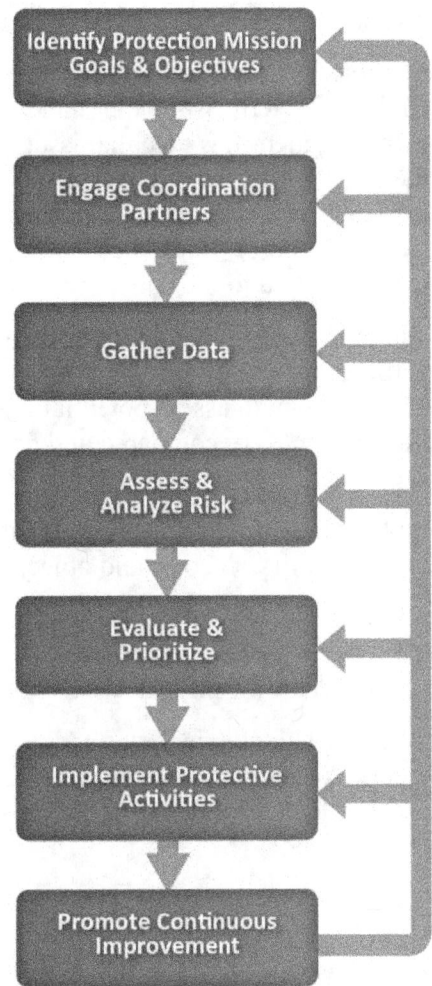

Figure 2: Steady-state Protection Process

1. **Identify Protection mission goals and objectives.** The initial step of the process is to identify exactly what the community or jurisdiction is trying to protect. Desired goals and objectives may vary across and within jurisdictions or areas of responsibility, depending on the risk landscape and operating environment. Goals and objectives that are collaboratively derived help establish a common vision of the desired long-term security posture and recovery criteria and should reflect the broad protection goals of the full range of partners. Protection partners also can draw on these goals during risk management to best determine which specific Protection core capabilities and risk-reduction and protective strategies most significantly enhance security in the area. Steps in the protection process should include identifying opportunities to build resilience into planning and implementation efforts.

2. **Engage partners.** This step of the protection cycle determines the size and scope of the community or jurisdiction's local coordinating structures by identifying additional protection

partners.[29] Protection partners will identify the core capabilities needed based on the Protection mission and delineate the roles and responsibilities for each protection partner.

3. **Gather data.** During this step, protection partners gather data concerning potential threats and hazards from international and domestic terrorism, other incidents, natural disasters, and infrastructure failures. Data gathering identifies potential issues, challenges, or vulnerabilities that may be associated with the specific activity or the size and scope of the Protection mission. The process involves research of current and historical information. Historical information is useful in assessing the possible likelihood of occurrence and consequences of potential threats and hazards. This information will be used to inform the risk assessment and other requirements.

4. **Assess and analyze risk.** During this step, protection partners assess and analyze risks to obtain a common risk picture. A specific methodology for the risk assessment is not prescribed.[30] Whatever the method used, it is important to assess potential threats, hazards, vulnerabilities, and consequences in a way that allows them to be compared and prioritized.

5. **Evaluate and prioritize.** In this step, protection partners use risk analysis results to evaluate their protection activities for potential risks. Partners also prioritize their Protection capability needs and efforts, taking into account mission goals and objectives.

6. **Implement protective activities.** In this step, protection partners identify the Protection core capabilities and resources needed to achieve the identified Protection goals and objectives. They implement protective activities to address the priorities established earlier in the process.

7. **Promote continuous improvement.** This step includes actions that ensure continuous improvement, such as training and exercising, identifying lessons learned, and reviewing evaluation results. This process may lead the community or jurisdiction to revisit any of the previous steps in the process.

Protection Escalation Decision Process

Interagency coordination may be compressed during periods of elevated threat or impending disasters. In this instance, communities move quickly to coordinate multiple jurisdictional protection activities (e.g., information sharing; interagency course of action development; communications planning/coordination; assessments, analysis, and modeling; alert and deployment of resources; and other activities required) in consultation and coordination with Federal departments and agencies and the affected jurisdiction(s). Figure 3 depicts this protection escalation decision process.

---

[29] Potential partners were described earlier in this section.

[30] For critical infrastructure security and resilience, the National Infrastructure Protection Plan provides criteria that need to be met for risk assessment methodologies. For additional information, refer to the National Infrastructure Protection Plan.

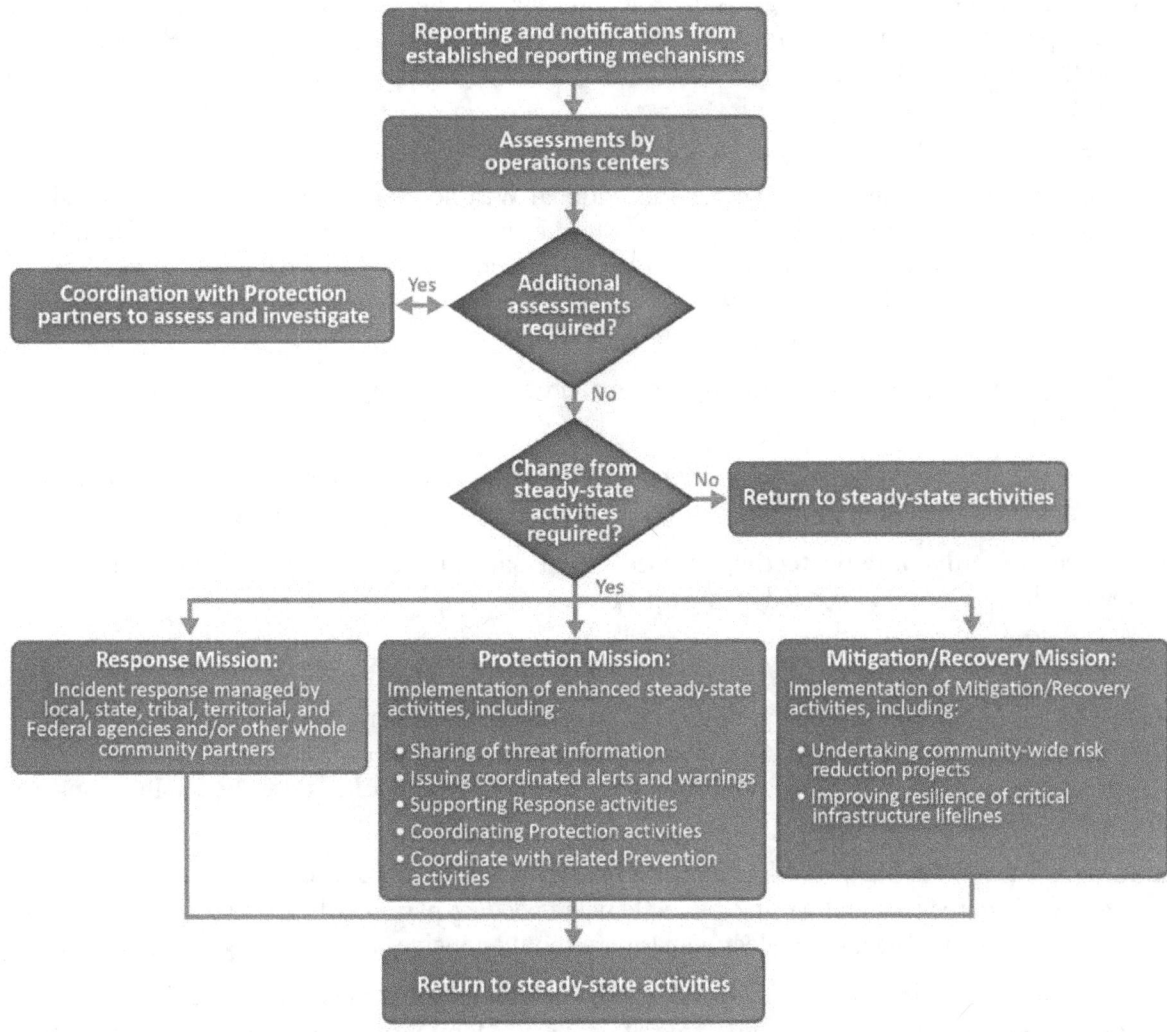

Figure 3: Protection Escalation Decision Process

- **Reporting and notifications.** The whole community shares information about potential threats and hazards using established communications and reporting channels. Depending on the type of threat or hazard, governmental, nongovernmental, and private sector organizations are either required or encouraged to report the potential threat and hazard information using existing mechanisms and legal requirements. Examples include law enforcement, health, and established partnership communications and reporting channels.

- **Assessments.** Governments at all levels maintain emergency operations, watch, and response centers to maintain situational awareness and analyze potential threats and consequences. An assessment of the emerging threat as credible and of the threat as exigent would signal a change from steady-state activities and require action in accordance with the National Response Framework, along with enhanced steady-state Protection and Mitigation activities. An assessment of the emerging threat as a potential terrorist threat may require action in accordance with the National Prevention Framework.

- **Response and enhanced steady-state protection activities.** Following an assessment of the situation, the situation may require the initiation of Response, Prevention, Mitigation, or

Recovery activities and a change from protection steady-state to enhanced steady-state activities. The importance of existing partnership structures and information sharing channels increases with the need for enhanced steady-state activities. Examples of protection activities taken during enhanced steady-state may include:

- Sharing of threat information including the issuances of watches, warnings, and other emergency bulletins. For example, the National Weather Service issues weather-related notices to warn the public of impending storms and severe weather. A number of health surveillance systems are used routinely at the national, state, and local levels to monitor health risks. The National Terrorism Advisory System communicates information about terrorist threats to the whole community.

- Supporting Response activities by making sure that communities and responders have adequate protection during the crisis.

- Coordinating with Prevention, Mitigation, Response, and Recovery activities through the implementation of appropriate authorities and the provision of resources.

- **Return to steady-state protection activities.** When an enhanced steady-state situation has abated, there is a return to steady-state activities.

Integration

Integration across the five mission areas results in synchronization and interoperability across the whole community. Integration is accomplished across and within the mission areas through planning and operational coordination processes, using the coordinating structures described in the respective frameworks and associated plans.

Planning. Protection entities coordinate planning activities across the whole community to ensure that required resources are and will be available when needed, particularly if those resources can be used to avert a threat or hazard. Protection partners should consider the following during planning:

- Estimating available resources from the whole community maximizes unity of effort and effectiveness, and reduces costs and time of delivery. Many jurisdictions, NGOs, and private sector organizations enter into mutual aid agreements to identify shared resources.

- Coordinating and analyzing requirements using common planning assumptions, risk assessments, or scenarios supports identifying which investments in capabilities most effectively address the threat or hazard and use resources most efficiently.

- Taking into consideration resource depletion rates incurred in previous or multiple events identifies potential gaps in resources over time.

Operational Coordination. The establishment and maintenance of unified operational structures and processes provides the architecture to appropriately integrate activities when required for the concurrent delivery of core capabilities for Prevention, Protection, Mitigation, Response, and Recovery. Joint training and exercising promotes integration and supports unity of effort by allowing Protection and other mission area partners to align coordination and communication structures.

Horizontal Integration

Protection partners integrate operations in the following ways:

- **Horizontal integration through partnerships and information sharing.** Protection core capabilities are coordinated across functional areas within a jurisdiction, such as police, fire, emergency medical services, public health, health systems, and public works entities. Core capabilities are also coordinated regionally with nearby jurisdictions that may share a common risk profile, resources, or information and support each other in delivering Protection core capabilities. Horizontal integration occurs between and among government entities and the private sector elements, community groups, faith-based organizations, and NGOs at all levels through partnerships and information sharing.

- **Horizontal integration through the frameworks and plans.** At the Federal level, horizontal integration is achieved across the five mission areas through the development of the frameworks, FIOPs,[31] and department-level operational plans. Specifically, all mission areas coordinate their frameworks with each other, focusing on integrating factors such as the core capabilities and the timing of overlapping activities. These factors are also applied in the development and maintenance of the FIOPs and Federal department-level operational plans. Using these integrating factors enables protection partners to understand the relationships, such as interdependencies and capabilities, among the five mission areas.

Vertical Integration

Vertical integration is a function of coordinating the implementation of core capabilities within the Protection mission area among the various sectors of the whole community. For example, states integrate their activities with local, tribal, and territorial jurisdictions, as well as with the Federal departments that support them in protection operations. Pertinent regional organizations are also included as essential elements of vertical integration; they can provide a bridge between the national and local levels.[32] In addition, all levels of government participate in joint protection exercises to ensure integration of their activities.

Relationship to Other Mission Areas

This section describes the relationship between Protection and the other mission areas. The National Protection Framework addresses steady-state and enhanced steady-state actions that require coordination and, for the most part, are carried out concurrently with those processes identified in the frameworks for Prevention, Mitigation, Response, and Recovery.

Prevention Mission Area

The **Prevention** and Protection mission areas are closely aligned, and overlap to some degree. Prevention includes the capabilities necessary to avoid, prevent, or stop a threatened or actual act of terrorism. As defined by PPD-8, for the purposes of the Frameworks the term "prevention" refers to preventing imminent threats from terrorism. The Prevention mission area focuses on those intelligence, technical, and law enforcement actions which prevent an adversary from carrying out an

---

[31] The FIOPs are a required component of the National Preparedness System directed under PPD-8. Their intent is to provide guidance across the Federal Government to successfully implement the frameworks.

[32] Examples of regional organizations include the PNWER Partnership, mentioned previously, and the All Hazards Consortium. The All Hazards Consortium facilitates regional integration among governments and private sector infrastructure owners and operators, primarily in the mid-Atlantic region of the United States.

attack within the United States when the threat is imminent. Protection activities, on the other hand, focus on government and private sector measures that deter terrorist actions or deter and disrupt other threats and hazards and, like mitigation, focus on minimizing the consequences of significant events. In some cases, the same capabilities that are used for protection functions are also used in prevention operations. However, while the National Prevention Framework addresses imminent acts of terrorism, the National Protection Framework addresses all hazards and the ongoing security of potential terrorist targets. Many other activities traditionally considered preventative, such as disease prevention and cybersecurity, fall under the Protection mission area based on the distinction between Prevention and Protection in PPD-8.

The National Protection and Prevention Frameworks share three of the same core capabilities. Processes described in these frameworks are designed to operate simultaneously and to provide for seamless integration when needed. For example, during a period of imminent terrorist threat, Prevention activities may focus on information sharing, law enforcement operations, and other activities to prevent, deter, and preempt terrorism. Protection may assess the increased risks and coordinates the information sharing and other actions needed to enhance specific protective measures.

Mitigation Mission Area

Mitigation refers to the capabilities necessary to reduce loss of life and property by lessening the impact and likelihood that a particular incident will result in a major disaster. Activities in the Mitigation and Protection mission areas typically are performed in a steady-state or well before an event. Protection places particular emphasis on security and deterring threats, while mitigation emphasizes achieving resilience by reducing vulnerabilities. Both seek to minimize consequences and have a nexus on critical infrastructure. Addressing the security of that infrastructure falls within the Protection mission area and the resilience of the infrastructure falls within the Mitigation mission area. Risk analysis is necessary to effectively design successful strategies for mitigation and protection. Integration of risk information, planning activities, and coordinating structures reduces duplication of effort and streamlines risk management actions in both mission areas.

Response Mission Area

The **Response** mission area includes the capabilities necessary to save lives, protect property and the environment, and meet basic human needs after an incident has occurred. Natural disasters and incidents can increase vulnerabilities that require the implementation during response activities of actions developed through the National Protection Framework. Efforts to protect people and communities as well as vital facilities, systems, and resources, are inextricably linked to response efforts. Responders support the Protection mission area and rely on protection organizations before, during, and after incidents. Protection resources and capabilities required to support response operations will be coordinated through the structures identified in the National Response Framework. The National Protection Framework provides the structure to assess and address increased vulnerabilities and risks beyond the specific disaster area and ensure that the protective posture is not compromised.

Recovery Mission Area

The **Recovery** mission area encompasses the capabilities necessary to assist communities affected by an incident to recover effectively. The systematic evaluation of the threats and hazards affecting the whole community and the executable strategies derived from that evaluation of the community's threats and hazards through risk-based planning are foundational to the actions taken during recovery. Coordination with the pre- and post-disaster recovery plans will ensure a resilient recovery process that takes protection into account. Protection and mitigation focus on a sustainable economy and community resilience and not just the swift restoration of infrastructure, buildings, and services.

Operational Planning

The National Planning Frameworks explain the role of each mission area in national preparedness and provide the overarching doctrine for how the whole community builds, sustains, and delivers the core capabilities. The concepts in the frameworks are used to guide operational planning, which provides further information regarding roles and responsibilities, identifies the critical tasks an entity will take in executing core capabilities, and identifies resourcing, personnel, and sourcing requirements. Operational planning is conducted across the whole community. At the Federal level, each framework is supported by a mission area-specific FIOP. Comprehensive Preparedness Guide 101 provides further information on the various types of plans and guidance on the fundamentals of planning.

The following sections outline how operational planning is applied within the Protection mission area at the Federal level.

Protection Operational Planning

Planning across the full range of protection activities is an inherent responsibility of every level of government, NGOs, and the private sector. A plan is a continuous, evolving instrument of anticipated or ongoing activities that maximizes opportunities and guides protection operations. Operational planning is conducted across the whole community. Its purpose is to determine jurisdictional priorities, objectives, strategies, and resource acquisitions and allocations needed to protect against potential threats, conduct law enforcement investigations, or engage in enforcement and protective activities based on jurisdictional authorities. From the Federal perspective, integrated planning helps explain how Federal departments and agencies and other national-level whole community partners provide the right resources at the right time to support local, state, tribal, territorial, and insular area operations.

Department-level Operational Plans

Each executive department and agency will develop and maintain deliberate department-level operational plans where needed, as determined by the respective department or agency, to deliver Protection core capabilities to fulfill the organization's responsibilities described in the FIOPs.

Departments and agencies may use existing plans, protocols, or standard operating procedures or guides for the development of such plans. Each department or agency determines its own planning requirements and decides whether its components or agencies need to develop subordinate operational plans.

Department-level operational plans identify specific critical tasks and responsibilities, including how to meet resource requirements and other specific provisions addressed in the FIOPs. Department-level operational plans also utilize the integrating factors for protection—addressing risk, planning and exercising coordination and communication procedures, and sharing resources—and Protection core capabilities.

Protection Federal Interagency Operational Plan

The Protection FIOP will describe how Federal departments and agencies work together to deliver the Protection core capabilities. Government, NGO, and private sector partners will be able to use the

Protection FIOP to inform ongoing protection planning, training, and exercising within their jurisdictions or organizations. The Protection FIOP will be developed through a collaborative process that ensures integration among all of the mission areas, with specific focus on Prevention and Mitigation. The information about Federal capabilities will enable government, NGO, and private sector partners to more accurately focus on local, state, tribal, territorial, and regional resource and capability requirements. Local, state, tribal, territorial, Federal, NGO, and private sector planning efforts supporting the National Protection Framework should address the following:

- Collaboration with all relevant stakeholders, including advocacy organizations or individuals with disabilities and others with access and functional needs, limited English proficiency, and ethnically and racially diverse groups
- A detailed concept of operations that explains how protection operations are coordinated and executed in a collaborative fashion[33]
- A description of critical tasks
- A description of roles and responsibilities
- Resource and personnel requirements
- Specific provisions for the rapid integration of resources and personnel for enhanced steady-state operations
- How protection plans may be executed simultaneously with other plans
- How the plan provides for multiple, geographically dispersed threats and hazards
- How the plan addresses the needs of impacted and medically vulnerable populations
- Compliance with provisions regarding the rights of individuals protected by civil rights laws, including individuals with disabilities, racial and ethnic minorities, and individuals with limited English proficiency.

In accordance with PPD-8, the Secretary of Homeland Security will coordinate the development of the Protection FIOP in collaboration with all Federal departments and agencies that play a role in the implementation of the core capabilities within the Protection mission area. The Roles and Responsibilities section identifies the Federal departments and agencies with predominant authorities or responsibilities within the Protection mission area. The departments and agencies identified have primary responsibility for engaging in the PPD-8 planning processes and engaging other Federal departments and agencies and others with relevant responsibilities. The Secretary of Homeland Security is responsible for the ongoing management and maintenance of the Protection FIOP. The Secretary will lead a process to review and update the Plan at least every three years or following major exercises, real-world events, or revisions to relevant authorities or doctrine.

Planning Assumptions

The following assumptions will guide the development of the operational plans:

- The capabilities of the whole community play a critical role in protection.

---

[33] A concept of operations is a statement that explains in broad terms what an organization (or group of organizations) intends to accomplish. It should describe how the organization or group will accomplish a set of objectives in order to reach a desired end-state.

- Activities within the Protection mission area occur continuously and may be implemented concurrently with Prevention, Mitigation, Response, and Recovery capabilities.

- The National Protection Framework focuses on steady-state and enhanced steady-state.

- Protection resources are acquired, allocated, and assigned through the normal Federal budget and program processes.

- Protection responsibilities are decentralized and command and control capabilities are distributed among Federal departments and agencies.

Framework Application

Government, NGO, and private sector partners can use the National Protection Framework to inform and align relevant planning, training, exercising, and other activities designed to enhance security for the whole community. The protection processes and guiding principles contained in this Framework provide a structured and unifying approach that is flexible and adaptable to specific Protection mission requirements. Focusing planning, training, and exercises on the Protection core capabilities enhances preparedness over the long term.

Supporting Resources

An array of resources is in place to support the Protection mission area. These resources include training, exercise, and web-based information—such as CitizenCorps.gov, USA.gov, and Ready.gov—that are available to both government and nongovernmental partners.

In addition, a variety of documents and guidelines exist that support the development of interagency and other operational plans. Examples include, but are not limited to: the National Infrastructure Protection Plan and related Sector-Specific Plans; Executive Order 13636: Improving Critical Infrastructure Cybersecurity; PPD-21: Critical Infrastructure Security and Resilience; National Security Presidential Directive 46: The U.S. Policy and Strategy in the War on Terror; Homeland Security Presidential Directive 5: Management of Domestic Incidents; the National Strategy for Global Supply Chain Security; and the Federal Interagency Geospatial Concept of Operations.

Conclusion

The shared responsibility for the Protection mission area builds from the individual level and the community level to local jurisdictions; state, tribal, and territorial governments; and the Federal Government. The National Protection Framework assists the whole community in protecting against the greatest risks to our Nation from all hazards in a manner that allows our interests, aspirations, and way of life to thrive.

The National Protection Framework provides the whole community with an understanding of the full spectrum of core capabilities within the Protection mission area and what they can do to ensure our Nation is optimally protected from manmade and natural disasters. Initiatives based on Protection core capabilities help guide a community to create conditions for a safer, more secure, and more resilient Nation by enhancing protection through cooperation and collaboration.

In implementing the National Protection Framework to build national preparedness, partners are encouraged to develop a shared understanding of broad-level strategic implications as they make critical decisions in building future capacity and capability. The whole community should be engaged in examining and implementing the unifying principles and doctrine contained in this Framework, considering both current and future requirements in the process. This means that this

Framework is a living document, and it will be regularly reviewed to evaluate consistency with existing and new policies, evolving conditions, and the experience gained from its use. The first review will be completed no later than 18 months after the release of this Framework. Subsequent reviews will be conducted in order to evaluate the effectiveness of this Framework on a quadrennial basis.

DHS will coordinate and oversee the review and maintenance process for the National Protection Framework. The revision process includes developing or updating any documents necessary to carry out capabilities. Significant updates to this Framework will be vetted through a Federal senior-level interagency review process. This Framework will be reviewed in order to accomplish the following:

- Assess and update information on the core capabilities in support of protection goals and objectives

- Ensure that it adequately reflects the organization of responsible entities

- Ensure that it is consistent with the other four mission areas

- Update processes based on changes in the national threat/hazard environment

- Incorporate lessons learned and effective practices from day-to-day operations, exercises, and actual incidents and alerts

- Reflect progress in the Nation's implementation of core capabilities within the Protection mission area, the need to execute new law, executive orders, and Presidential directives, as well as strategic changes to national priorities and guidance, critical tasks, or national capabilities.

The implementation and review of the National Protection Framework will consider effective practices and lessons learned from exercises and operations, as well as pertinent new processes and technologies. Effective practices include continuity planning, which ensures that the capabilities contained in this Framework can continue to be executed regardless of the threat or hazard. Pertinent new processes and technologies should enable the Nation to adapt efficiently to the evolving risk environment and use data relating to location, context, and interdependencies that allow for effective integration across all missions using a standards-based approach.

America's security and resilience work is never finished. While the Nation is safer, stronger, and better prepared than a decade ago, the commitment to safeguard the Nation against the greatest risks it faces, now and for decades to come, remains resolute. By bringing the whole community together now to support the collective and integrated action needed to address the shared future needs, the Nation will continue to improve its preparedness to face whatever challenges unfold.